Pupil Book 6

Spelling

Author: Chris Whitney

William Collins' dream of knowledge for all began with the publication of his first book in 1819. A self-educated mill worker, he not only enriched millions of lives, but also founded a flourishing publishing house. Today, staying true to this spirit, Collins books are packed with inspiration, innovation and practical expertise. They place you at the centre of a world of possibility and give you exactly what you need to explore it.

Collins. Freedom to teach.

Published by Collins
An imprint of HarperCollins*Publishers*
The News Building
1 London Bridge Street
London
SE1 9GF

Browse the complete Collins catalogue at
www.collins.co.uk

© HarperCollins*Publishers* Limited 2015

10 9 8 7 6 5 4 3 2 1

ISBN 978-0-00-813337-5

British Library Cataloguing in Publication Data
A Catalogue record for this publication is available from the British Library

Edited by Jessica Marshall
Cover design and artwork by Amparo Barrera
Internal design concept by Amparo Barrera
Typesetting by Jouve India Private Ltd
Illustrations by Aptara and QBS

Printed in Italy by Grafica Veneta S.p.A.

Pupil Book 6
Spelling

Contents

	Page
Unit 1: The suffixes -cious and -tious	6
Unit 2: The suffixes -cial and -tial	8
Unit 3: The suffixes -ant, -ance / -ancy, -ent and -ence / -ency	10
Unit 4: The suffixes -able, -ible, -ably and -ibly	12
Unit 5: Adding suffixes beginning with vowel letters to words ending in -fer	14
Unit 6: Use of the hyphen after prefixes	16
Unit 7: The ee sound spelt ei after c	18
Unit 8: The letter-string ough	20
Unit 9: Words with 'silent' letters	22
Unit 10: Homophones and near-homophones (1)	24
Unit 11: Homophones and near-homophones (2)	26
Unit 12: Homophones and near-homophones (3)	28
Unit 13: Homophones and near-homophones (4)	30
Unit 14: Homophones and near-homophones (5)	32

The suffixes -cious and -tious

The ending **-ious** can be added to turn nouns into adjectives. If the root word ends in **-ce**, the ending is **-cious**.

Remove the e before adding **-ious**: grace + ious = gra**cious**.

If the root word ends in **-tion**, the ending is **-tious**.

Remove the **-ion** before adding **-ious**: caution + ious = cau**tious**. There is one common exception: anx**ious**.

Get started

Sort these words into nouns and adjectives by looking at the word endings. Copy and complete the table. One has been done for you.

1. infectious

2. conscious

3. caution

4. infection

5. space

6. fictitious

7. cautious

8. spacious

9. grace

10. avarice

Nouns	Adjectives
	infectious

Try these

Choose the correct spelling of each word. One has been done for you.

1. spatious / spacious

   Answer: *spacious*

2. malicious / malitious

3. nutricious / nutritious

4. pretencious / pretentious

5. contencious / contentious

Copy and complete the sentences by choosing the correct spelling of each word. One has been done for you.

1. *Sumo wrestlers must have <u>voracious</u> appetites. (voracious / voratious)*

2. Liza never walks under ladders: she is _____. (supersticious / superstitious)

3. The greedy millionaire was an _____ man. (avaricious / avaritious)

4. My brother is always a _____ host. (gracious / gratious)

5. Be _____ when handling deadly snakes. (caucious / cautious)

Now try these

Change each noun to an adjective and use it in a sentence of your own. One has been done for you.

ambition, malice, nutrition, pretention, contention, vice, auspice, caprice, office, fraction

Answer: *Seth's plan to sail around the world was ambitious.*

The suffixes -cial and -tial

Some words end with the suffixes **-cial** and **-tial**. After a vowel, we usually use the ending **-cial**, for example: spa**cial**. After a consonant, we usually use the ending **-tial**, for example: torren**tial**.

Get started

Sort these words into two groups: words that are spelt correctly and words that are not spelt correctly. Copy and complete the table. One has been done for you.

1. artificial

2. quintessential

3. confidential

4. parcial

5. unoffitial

6. facial

7. potencial

8. superficial

9. artificial

10. antisotial

Correct	Incorrect
artificial	

Try these

Add the correct suffixes to the following root words. Look carefully at the final letter of the root word before you make your decision. One has been done for you.

1. *crucial*
2. poten
3. mar
4. spe
5. benefi
6. essen
7. substan
8. par

Now try these

Copy and complete the paragraphs by choosing the correct words. One has been done for you.

For Sandeep, it was <u>*crucial*</u> that he win this game of table tennis.

A p_____l victory was not enough; he wanted the o_____l title of champion. He had his s_____l lucky bat in his hand. "Today has the p_____l to be a great day," said Sandeep.

Exercise is e_____l to keeping fit. Training in m_____l arts could make a s_____l improvement to your fitness and may also be b_____l to your s_____l life.

The suffixes -ant, -ance / -ancy, -ent and -ence / -ency

The endings **-ant** and **-ent** sound similar. Use **-ant** if there is a related word with an **ay** sound in the right position. The ending **-ation** is often a clue. For example: hesi**tation** – hesi**tant**.

Use **-ent** after the soft **c** sound, after the soft **g** sound, or if there is a related word with a clear **e** sound in the right position. For example: inno**cent**, ag**ent**, confidential – confid**ent**.

There are many words, however, that just have to be learned. For example: assist**ant**, obedi**ent** and independ**ent**.

Get started

Sort these words into two groups: words that end in **-ance / -ancy** and words that end in **-ence / -ency**. Copy and complete the table. One has been done for you.

1. infancy	2. residence
3. currency	4. occupancy
5. expectancy	6. fluency
7. emergence	8. observance

-ance / -ancy	-ence / -ency
infancy	

Try these

Copy and complete the table by adding the correct suffix to each root word to make the related adjectives and nouns. Listen to the final sound in the root word. One has been done for you.

Root	Adjective	Noun
negli**g**	*negligent*	*negligence*
magnific		
extravag		
eleg		
urg		
converg		

Now try these

Copy and complete the sentences by writing the correct spelling of each word. One has been done for you.

1. *Mary was happy: at last she had her driving lic<u>ence</u>.*

2. Ashley was confid_____ that she would pass the history test.

3. From the top of the mountain, there was a magnific_____ view.

4. The fire alarm rang with a sense of urg_____.

5. Chickens are not renowned for their intellig_____.

6. The soldier conducted himself with dec_____ and honour.

7. Though ineleg_____ on land, penguins are very eleg_____ underwater.

8. There is evid_____ that monkeys are very intellig_____ animals.

The suffixes -able, -ible, -ably and -ibly

Some adjectives end with the suffixes **-able** or **-ible**. Their related adverbs end with the suffixes **-ably** or **-ibly**.

Usually, the **-able** / **-ably** ending is used if a complete root word can be heard before it. If there is no complete root word, then use **-ible** / **-ibly**. For example: **depend**able / **depend**ably, **poss**ible / **poss**ibly.

The **-able** / **-ably** endings are also used if there is a related word ending in **-ation**. For example: ador**able** / ador**ably** / ador**ation**.

If the root word ends in **y**, it usually becomes **i** before the suffix. For example: re**ly** / reli**able**. However, there are exceptions to this. For example: enjo**y** / enjoy**able**.

If the root word ends in **e**, the **e** is removed before adding **-able** / **-ably**. For example: admir**e** / admir**able** / admir**ably**. However, if the root word ends in **-ce** or **-ge**, then the **e** is **not** removed. For example: chang**e** / chang**eable**.

When the endings **-ible** and **-ibly** are added to words ending in **-e**, **-ce** or **-ge**, the **e** is removed. For example: forc**e** / forc**ible** / forc**ibly**.

Get started

Change each verb into an adverb by adding the correct suffix. One has been done for you.

1. applicable

   Answer: *applicably*

2. comfort

3. accept

4. understand

5. notice

6. fashion

Try these

Change each verb into an adjective by adding the correct suffix. Look carefully at the verb endings. One has been done for you.

1. consider

   Answer: *considerable*

2. collapse

3. vary

4. manage

5. response

6. imagine

7. sense

8. change

Now try these

Copy and complete the sentences by choosing the correct spelling for each word. One has been done for you.

1. 'This film was <u>*arguably*</u> the best this year,' typed Samir in his email. (arguably / argueably)

2. Manuel is the most _____ bachelor in town. (eligeable / eligible)

3. The Mayor was persuaded by _____ protest. (forceible / forcible)

4. Many plastics are _____: they do not snap when bent. (pliable / plyable)

5. To Georgia, her old teddy bear was _____. (irreplacable / irreplaceable)

6. The advertisement for sky diving claimed the risks were _____. (negligeable / negligible)

7. A _____ boat is called a submarine. (submergeible / submergible)

8. Charlene's messy handwriting is _____. (illegeable / illegible)

9. The tension in the atmosphere was almost _____. (tangeible / tangible)

Adding suffixes beginning with vowels to words ending in –fer

When you add a suffix that starts with a vowel (for example, **-ed** or **-ing**) to a word ending in **-fer**, the spelling rule depends on which syllable is stressed.

If the **second** syllable is stressed, double the **r** when adding the suffix.
If the second syllable is **not** stressed, do not double the **r.**

Get started

Add **-ed** to these words and decide if the **r** should be doubled or not. One has been done for you.

1. proffer

    Answer: *proffered*

2. buffer

3. pilfer

4. differ

5. defer

Listen to whether or not the **-fer** syllable is stressed after adding the suffix. Sort the words into two groups: words where **-fer** is stressed and words where it is not. Copy and complete the table.

-fer is stressed when the suffix is added	-fer is not stressed when the suffix is added

Try these

Add **-ing** and **-ence** to these words, and decide if the **r** should be doubled or not. Copy and complete the table. One has been done for you.

Verb	Add -ing	Add -ence
confer	*conferring*	*conference*
transfer		
refer		
defer		
differ		
infer		

Now try these

Copy and complete the paragraph by choosing the correct spelling for each word. One has been done for you.

When Adam saw Mr Whiskers in a tree, he _inferred_ that he was stuck and climbed up to rescue him. Unfortunately, Adam s_____d from a fear of heights, normally p_____g to stay on the ground. (In this, Adam and Mr Whiskers d_____d greatly – Mr Whiskers actually p_____d high places.) Adam was o_____d help by a firefighter who said: "What a pickle," r_____g to Adam's situation. After c_____g with Adam, the firefighter suggested t_____g Adam's weight from the tree to his shoulders. Adam was terrified but eventually d_____d to the firefighter's better judgement and was rescued.

Use of the hyphen after prefixes

Hyphens can be used to join a prefix to a root word, if adding it helps the reader with pronunciation or meaning. If the prefix ends in a vowel and the root word begins with a vowel, the hyphen tells the reader to say two separate syllables.

Get started

Insert the hyphen in each word to help with pronunciation. One has been done for you.

1. ultraangry

   Answer: *ultra-angry*

2. coown

3. antiageing

4. reeducate

5. reenter

6. deice

7. reelect

8. coordinate

9. cooperate

10. preelection

Try these

Choose the correct spelling for each word. One has been done for you.

1. pre-election / preelection

   Answer: *pre-election*

2. re-enter / reenter

3. re-accumulate / reaccumulate

4. non-sense / nonsense

5. re-educate / reeducate

6. anti-freeze / antifreeze

7. de-frost / defrost

8. co-educate / coeducate

9. co-ordinate / coordinate

10. re-bound / rebound

Now try these

Use each of your answers from 'Try these' in a sentence of your own. One has been done for you.

Answer: *The batsman hit the ball on the* <u>*rebound*</u>.

The ee sound spelt ei after c

The rhyme 'i before e, except after **c**' can help you to spell the **ee** sound. After **c**, the letters that make the **ee** sound are the other way around: **e** comes before **i**. There are a number of exceptions to the rule. These exceptions just need to be learned.

Get started

Sort these words into two groups: those that follow the rule '**i** before **e** except after **c**' and those that do not follow the rule. One has been done for you.

1. niece

2. protein

3. conceive

4. weird

5. caffeine

6. neither

7. receive

8. either

9. seize

10. friend

Words that follow the rule	Words that do not follow the rule
niece	

Try these

Copy and complete the sentences by putting the jumbled letters in the correct order to spell the missing word. One has been done for you.

1. *On Monday, I will visit my <u>niece</u>, Chloe.* (eenci)

2. The _____ constable is a severe but reasonable man. (cfeih)

3. I am too trusting: I _____ everything I'm told. (elbeevi)

4. I challenge you to a duel, you lying, _____ scoundrel! (udeeflict)

5. Kitchens should always be clean and _____. (ihngeicy)

6. John lay on his bed and stared up at the _____. (nicegli)

7. The kitten was always causing _____. (ihsmfice)

8. The castle had been under _____ for many months. (igese)

9. On your birthday, it is usual to _____ gifts. (creeiev)

10. It was autumn and the corn had turned golden in the _____. (ledfis)

Now try these

Use each of the following words in a sentence of your own. One has been done for you.

relieved, mischievous, receipt, deceive, perceive, conceited, piece, achieve, retrieve, shriek

Answer: *After days apart, the cub was <u>relieved</u> to see his mother again.*

The letter-string ough

The letter-string **ough** is one of the trickiest spellings in English. It can be used to spell a number of different sounds.

For example: He had a nasty **cough**. (Here, **ough** rhymes with **off**.)

The baker threw the dough onto the table. (Here, **ough** rhymes with **no**.)

Get started

Find the misspelt words in each set – some have more than one. One has been done for you.

1. rough, ruff, ruph

   Answer: *ruph*

2. stough, stuff, stuph

3. coff, cow, cough

4. bough, bau, bow,

5. wow, wough, woe

6. thorough, corough, borough

7. doe, dow, dough,

8. through, threw, threu

9. trough, troff, troph

10. blue, blew, blough

Try these

There are ten misspelt words in this paragraph. Copy the paragraph and correct the spellings – they should all be spelt with **ough**. One has been done for you.

The harvest had been safely ~~brort~~ *brought* in by the people of the **burah**. "Perhaps I **ort** to **plow** the fields now," the farmer **thort** as she filled the cow's feeding **troff**, "winter is coming and the weather is getting **ruff**." The old apple tree had already lost one of its **bows** in the autumn wind and, **althow** there had been a **drowt** all summer, now it looked like rain.

Now try these

Use each of the following words in a sentence of your own. One has been done for you.

brought, sought, thought, although, cough, trough, dough, rough, through, tough

Answer: *Paolo <u>brought</u> his new toy to school.*

Words with 'silent' letters

'Silent' letters are the letters you cannot detect from the way a word is pronounced. They exist because the pronunciation of many words in the English language has changed over time. Some letters are no longer pronounced, even though they still exist in the spellings.

Get started

Add letters to each of these words to correct the spellings. One has been done for you.

1. stomac

   Answer: *stomach*

2. sutle

3. rinkle

4. receit

5. condem

6. ryme

7. colum

8. nickers

9. bom

10. clim

Try these

Find the correctly spelt word(s) in each set – some have more than one. One has been done for you.

1. wayle, whale, wail

   Answer: *whale, wail*

2. plum, plumb, plumn

3. gnaw, nor, knaw

4. write, wriht, right

5. kneel, gneel, kneil

6. gnot, not, knot

7. knome, nohme, gnome

8. answer, ansher, arnser

9. island, aisland, iyland

10. limb, limp, limn

Now try these

Copy and complete the paragraph by finding twelve misspelt words and correcting the spellings. (They are all missing their silent letters.) One has been done for you.

The **night** *knight* dismounted and unbuckled his **sord**. Exhausted, he rested a **wile** by an old **narled** oak tree and **restled** with his conscience. Night was approaching, his **nee** was wounded and his **stomac** was empty. He wanted to rest but, if he stopped, he might be too late to save the King, who he had sworn a **solem** oath to protect. He clenched his **nuckles** and **nashed** his teeth with frustration. If only he **new wat** to do.

Homophones and near-homophones (1)

Homophones are words that sound the same but are spelt differently and have different meanings. You always need context (a setting, for example a sentence) to know which spelling to use. Often, the spellings of homophones just have to be learned.

Near-homophones are words that sound similar. They are also spelt differently and have different meanings.

Get started

Match each of these words to the correct synonym. One has been done for you.

desert, dessert, wary, weary, affect, effect, complement, compliment, precede, proceed

1. tired

   Answer: *weary*

2. progress

3. cautious

4. abandon

5. influence

6. pre-exist

7. consequence

8. pudding

9. addition

10. flatter

Try these

Copy and complete each sentence by choosing the correct word to fill in the gap. One has been done for you.

1. *The teacher <u>complimented</u> David on his work.* (complemented / complimented)

2. The parade _____ across the square to the Town Hall. (proceeded / preceded)

3. This terrible tragedy has _____ us all. (affected / effected)

4. Last night's storm _____ this morning's floods. (proceeded / preceded)

5. All _____ from the cake sale will go to charity. (proceeds / precedes)

6. At high noon, the sheriff found the streets _____. (desserted / deserted)

7. It was Marek's birthday so she had two _____ after her lunch! (desserts / deserts)

8. The man is infamous: his reputation _____ him. (proceeds / precedes)

Now try these

Write a sentence for each of these words. You can use prefixes and suffixes, but make sure the root is correct for the context. One has been done for you.

desert, dessert, wary, weary, affect, effect, complement, compliment, precede, proceed

Answer: *Jana's blue headband <u>complements</u> her eyes perfectly.*

Homophones and near-homophones (2)

Homophones are words that sound the same, but they are spelt differently and have different meanings. You always need context to know how to spell homophones. Some homophone pairs can be told apart because one of the words is a past-tense verb.

Get started

Match each word to the correct synonym. One has been done for you.

guessed, lead, past, guest, herd, led

1. estimated

   Answer: *guessed*

2. visitor

3. group

4. history

5. escorted

6. metal

In your own words, write a definition for each of these words. Use a dictionary if you need to. One has been done for you.

7. herd: *a group of animals*

8. passed

9. lead

10. heard

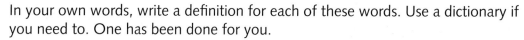

Try these

Copy and complete each sentence, choosing the correct word to fill the gap. One has been done for you.

1. *Matilda guessed all the answers in her spelling test.* (guest / guessed)

2. I can't dance: it's as though my feet are made of _____. (led / lead)

3. Fast asleep in baby bear's bed was an uninvited _____. (guest / guessed)

4. I've _____ it's very pleasant in Italy at this time of year. (herd / heard)

5. I _____ my swimming test with excellent marks! (past / passed)

6. The dog _____ the man to where the children were trapped. (led / lead)

7. The guide tried to _____ the tourists towards the exit. (herd / heard)

8. In the _____, wolves lived and thrived in Britain. (past / passed)

Now try these

Write a sentence for each of these words. One has been done for you.

guessed, guest, passed, past, led, lead, heard, herd (noun), herd (verb)

Answer: *On the drive home, the family passed a river.*

Homophones and near-homophones (3)

Homophones are words that sound the same, but are spelt differently and have different meanings.

Some homophone pairs can be told apart because one of the words is a verb and the other is a noun. For example, **practice** (with a **c**) is a noun meaning 'a custom or procedure' such as in the sentence: 'Prayer is a practice observed by many religions'. **Practise** (with an **s**) is a verb and means: 'to repeat something in order to improve' as in the sentence: 'Carl practises the piano every day'.

Get started

Match a word to the correct synonym. There are two extra words. One has been done for you.

advice, license, advise, device, licence, prophecy, devise, practise, prophesy, practice

1. a permit

   Answer: *licence*

2. predict

3. invent

4. allow

5. suggest

6. carry out

7. recommendation

8. appliance

Try these

Decide whether each word is a verb or a noun and write a definition for each word. Use a dictionary if you need to. One has been done for you.

1. practice: *(noun)* *a custom or procedure*

2. advise: (_____)

3. prophecy: (_____)

4. licence: (_____)

5. prophesy: (_____)

6. devise: (_____)

7. practise: (_____)

8. license: (_____)

9. advice: (_____)

10. device: (_____)

Now try these

Write a sentence for each of these words. Use prefixes and suffixes if you want to but make sure the root is correct for the context. One has been done for you

practice, practise, licence, license, prophecy, prophesy, advice, advise, device, devise

Answer: *Vijay* _practised_ *his singing until he had the voice of an angel.*

Homophones and near-homophones (4)

Homophones are words that sound the same, but are spelt differently and have different meanings. You always need context to know how to spell homophones. Often, the spellings of homophones just have to be learned.

Get started

Write a synonym for each of these words, using a dictionary if you need to. One has been done for you.

1. draft

Answer: *outline*

2. principal

3. aisle

4. principle

5. isle

6. serial

7. aloud

8. draught

9. allowed

10. stationary

11. cereal

12. stationery

Try these

Copy and complete each sentence, choosing the correct word to fill the gap.
One has been done for you.

1. *For breakfast, Kyle and his dad always ate <u>cereal</u>.* (cereal / serial)

2. Children are not _____ near the water's edge. (aloud / allowed)

3. Envelopes are kept in the _____ cupboard. (stationary / stationery)

4. The _____ of Man is part of the United Kingdom. (Aisle / Isle)

5. The _____ of the school welcomed the new pupils.
(principal / principle)

6. If you have a good idea, please speak your thoughts _____.
(aloud / allowed)

7. The bride tripped on her dress as she walked down the _____.
(aisle / isle)

8. Every Monday, Aleksy watched his favourite television _____.
(cereal / serial)

9. Unmoving, unblinking, the tiger remained entirely _____.
(stationary / stationery)

10. It is against my _____ to lie, cheat or swindle. (principals / principles)

Now try these

Write a sentence for each of these words. Use prefixes
and suffixes if you want to but make sure the root is
correct for the context. One has been done for you.

aisle, isle, serial, cereal, aloud, allowed, draft, draught,
stationary, stationery

Answer: *In this supermarket, cleaning products
are found in <u>aisle</u> three.*

Homophones and near-homophones (5)

Homophones are words that sound the same, but are spelt differently and have different meanings. You always need context (a setting, for example a sentence) to know how to spell homophones. Often, the spellings of homophones just have to be learned. For example, **bridle**: headgear for controlling a horse; **bridal**: of or relating to a bride.

Get started

Sort these words into their different word types – some of them fit into more than one category. Copy and complete the table, using a dictionary if you need to. One has been done for you.

1. ascent

2. bridle

3. descent

4. morning

5. father

6. bridal

7. mourning

8. profit

9. farther

10. prophet

Nouns	Verbs	Adjectives	Adverbs
mourning	*mourning*		

Try these

Write a definition for each of these words, using a dictionary if you need to. One has been done for you.

1. assent: *an agreement or to agree*

2. steel

3. morning

4. dissent

5. steal

6. mourning

7. ascent

8. whose

9. descent

10. who's

Now try these

Write a sentence for each of these words. Use prefixes and suffixes if you want to but make sure the root is correct for the context. One has been done for you.

whose, who's, ascent, assent, descent, dissent, father, farther, morning, mourning, steal, steel, bridal, bridle, profit, prophet

Answer: *"Whose smelly socks are these?" asked Mum.*